Let's Crochet a HAT

KEKE HUDSON

Archway Publishing books may be ordered through booksellers or by contacting:

Archway Publishing
1663 Liberty Drive
Bloomington, IN 47403
www.archwaypublishing.com
844-669-3957

Interior Image Credit: Keke L Hudson

ISBN: 978-1-6657-3383-0 (sc)
ISBN: 978-1-6657-3384-7 (e)

Print information available on the last page.

Archway Publishing rev. date: 12/07/2022

"I can do all things through Christ who strengthens me!" Pilli 4:13 (Kings James Version)

Dedicated to my heart and souls! For all things are possible even when the light seems dull.

Crochet has been around for centuries. It is a process of handcrafting yarn into a patterned or textile fabric, by looping yarn using a hooked needle.

Here is a simple halter top I made for the summer!

Crochet is often mistake for knitting, because they both use a special type of needle. The best and easy way to remember the difference between the two styles is to think of it as a number. In crochet we use one single hooked needle, and when knitting we use two straight needles without a hook. Both methods are used to create beautiful patterned pieces.

Photo taken to show the difference between the needles.

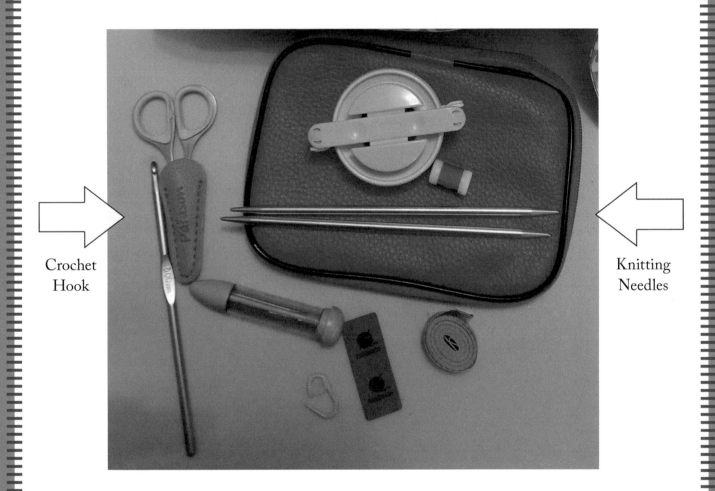

Crochet
Hook

Knitting
Needles

In case this is your first time crocheting. A crochet hook comes in many different sizes, and are used to make many different things. For example some crochet hooks can range from size 2.0 mm to 10mm. The smaller the hook the thinner the yarn will be. The thicker the yarn, the larger the hook will be.

In the set below, the hooks range from small to large and will vary in each set.

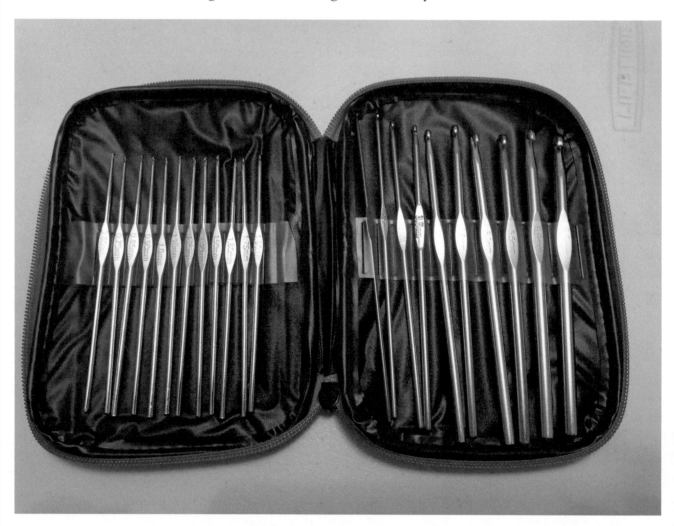

Hook sizes 0.60 mm to 6.5 mm

In order to begin your first crochet, below are the steps and images to a few simple basic stitches that, will help you along the way. Practice each step over and over until you get it. If you mess up keep trying don't give up!

The first stitch we will learn is called the foundation chain. This chain is the very beginning of your project, you can think of it like a building block. Without your foundation block, there is nothing to build off of. So when we crochet this step is the most important step in order to build a project.

Foundation Chain

Step 1

Wrap yarn around your index finger. As show in the image.

 Step 2

Holding the short end of the yarn. Hold yarn in place with your thumb. As shown in the image.

Step 3

Pull short end through the loop as shown in the image.

 Step 4

Pull loop up and tight to make a knot. This knot is also called a slip knot, or a sliding knot.

Step 5

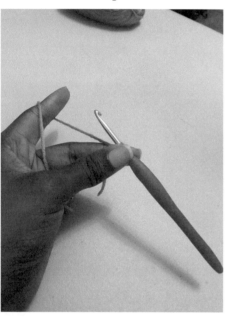

Put the hook through the loop and, wrap the yarn over your index finger as shown in the image.

Step 6

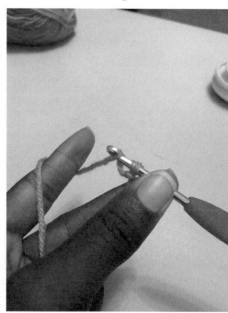

YO (Yarn Over)

Wrap the yarn over the hook and pull through the loop.

Step 7

First foundation chain stitch made. Repeat step 7 for second chain stitch.

Step 8

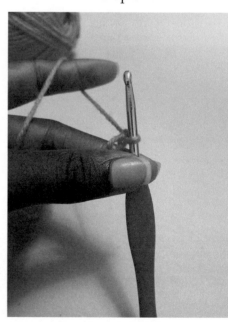

First foundation chain stitch made. Repeat step 7 for second chain stitch.

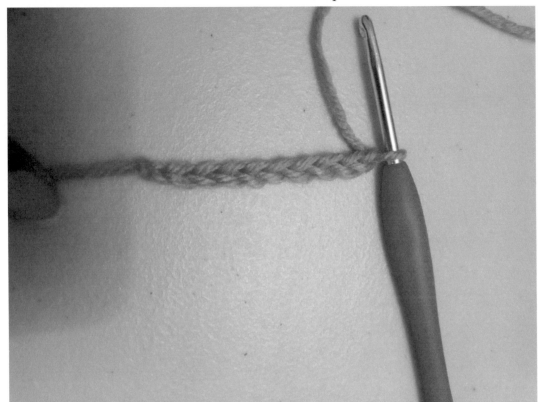

Repeat steps 1-9 for a total of 10 chain stitches. Repeat if necessary.

Single Crochet

Step 1

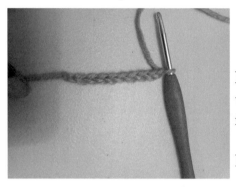

Insert hook into the 2nd chain space from your hook.

Pull up a loop.

2nd chain space

Step 2

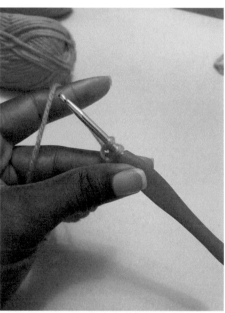

Now with 2 loops on you hook. Pull through both loops to complete your single crochet stitch.

Repeat steps 1-2. Your chain should now look like this. Repeat if necessary.

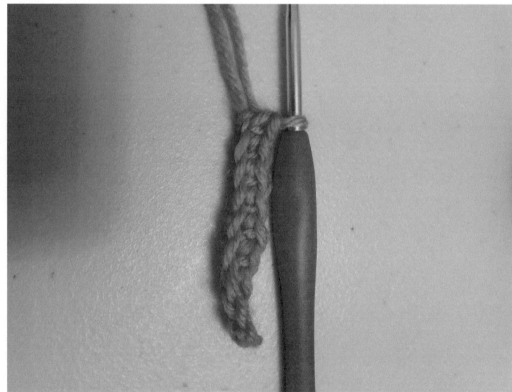

Half Double Crochet

Step 1

Wrap your yarn over your hook, and pull through all 3 loops half double crochet stitch made.

Step 2

Insert hook into the 2nd chain space and pull up a loop.

You should now have 3 loops on your hook, as shown.

Step 4

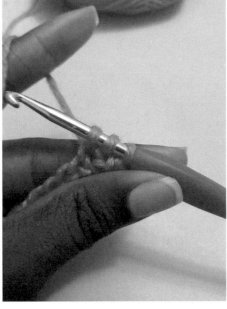

Wrap your yarn over your hook, and pull through all 3 loops half double crochet stitch made.

Step 5

Completed half double crochet

Repeat if necessary

Double Crochet Stitch

Step 1

Make a foundation chain of 10. As shown in the image above.

Step 2

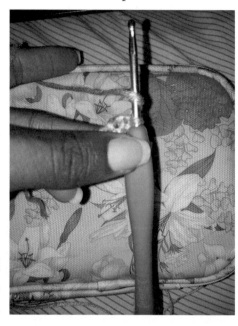

Wrap the yarn around your hook. As shown in the image above.

Step 3

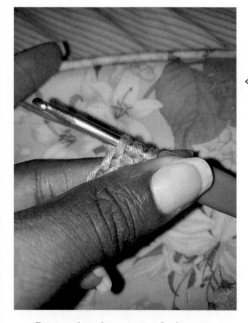

Insert hook into 2nd chain from hook and pull up a loop.

You will know have 3 loops on your hook.

Step 4

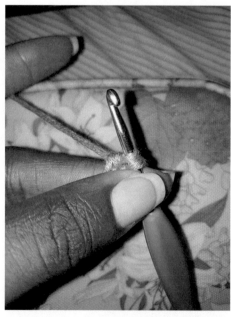

Wrap your yarn over your hook and pull through 2 loops. As shown in the image above.

Step 5

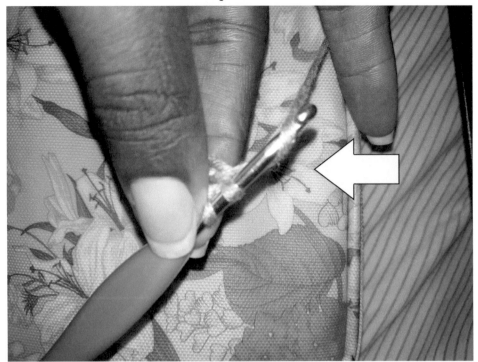

Wrap yarn around hook and pull through remaining 2 loops on your hook.

Step 6

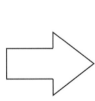

Repeat steps 1-5 till the end of your chain.

Repeat if necessary.

Now that you have learned how to make basic crochet stitches, lets make a magic circle, so you can begin your first crochet hat project. Below is a list of materials needed to make your hat.

MATERIALS

- H/8 or 5.00 mm hook, any kind.
- 1 skein of your favorite yarn, or any brand of yarn you may like.
- tapestry needle to weave in ends.
- Stitch marker
- Scissors

1 skein of yarn

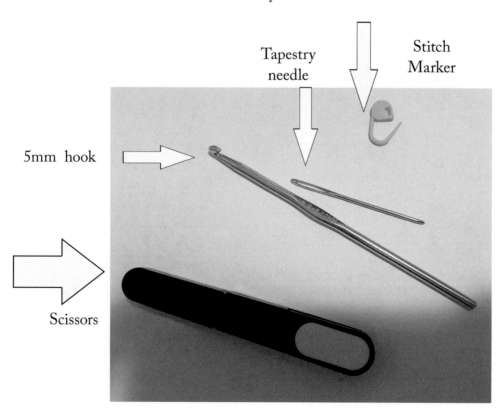

5mm hook

Tapestry needle

Stitch Marker

Scissors

Magic Circle

Step 1

Wrap yarn around your your four fingers.

As shown in the image.

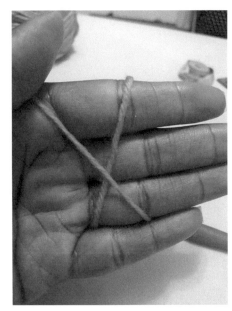

Step 2

Using the short tail of the yarn pull up and making an X.

Hold in position with your thumb.

As shown in the image.

Step 3

Holding the short end of the tail with you thumb keeping your x together.

Insert your hook under your first loop of the x and on top of the second loop.

As shown in the image.

Step 4

Pull up the second loop
with your hook.
Your yarn will twist with a
loop remaining on your hook.

Hold loop together
with your thumb.

Step 5

Remove the loop from your
fingers as shown in the image.

Hold together with your
thumb and open with
your index finger.

As shown in the image.

Step 6

Holding the loop you made pinch the top of your loop closed using your thumb.

Keep hook in the top loop of your circle. As shown in the image

Step 7

With your hook in the loop yarn over pull up a loop.

Insert hook into magic circle and pull up another loop.

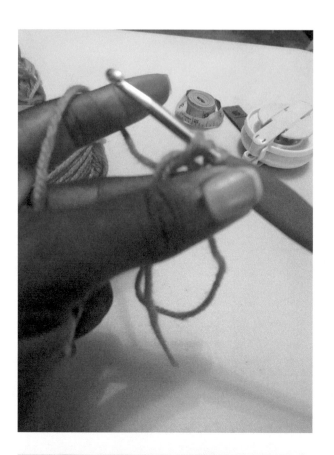

Step 8

Pull through all 3
loops on your hook
For your first half
double crochet made
in the magic circle.

As shown in the image.

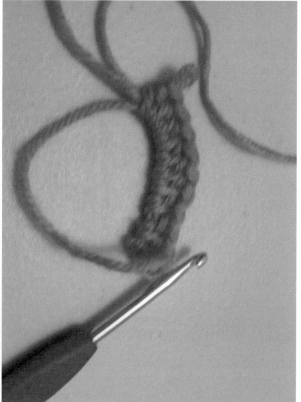

Step 9

Crochet 15 hdc in the ring for
a child and 18 for an adult hat.

As shown in the image.

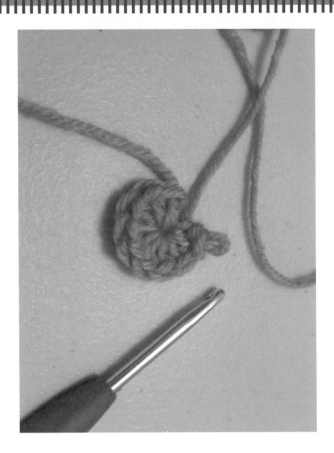

Step 10

Pull the short end of the tail to cinch circle closed.

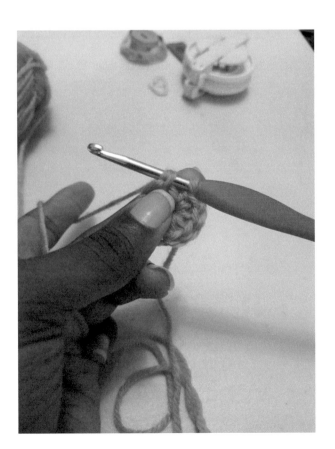

Step 11

To slip stitch loop closed insert loop into last stitch of your circle.

Wrap yarn around your hoop and pull through both loops on your hook.

Step 12a

Wrap yarn over your
hook and chain 2

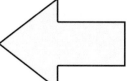

Chain 2
space

Step 12b

Chain 2 at the end of each
round as shown in the image.

Step 13

Round 2 : this is your
increase row. Put 2 hdc in
each stitch in your round.

This will increase your stitch
count from 15 to 30 if your
making a hat for a child.

If your making a hat for
an adult your stitch count
will increase from 18 to 36
stitches. Slip stitch at the
end of your row and chain 2

Tip

If your a beginner at crochet,
it is very beneficial to use a
stitch marker to help keep track
of each rounds you make.

If you don't have a stitch
marker on hand such as the
one shown in the image.

It is okay to use a piece
of yarn of a different
color or a paper clip.

Step 14

Round 3-4 are your increase rows.

The chain 2 space at the end of your rounds does not count as a stitch.

To increase 1 hdc in the next stitch 2 hdc in the next, repeat.

1 hdc, 2 hdc, 1 hdc, 2, hdc till the end of your round chain 2 (Repeat)

Step 15

Rounds 5-17 (child's hat)
Rounds 5-20 (adults hat)

1 hdc in each stitch around slip stitch at the end of your round, chain 2

Repeat for 12 rounds for the child's hat and 15 rounds for an adults hat.

Step 16

Just as shown in this image of the adult hat, keep

growing your hat by continuing your half double crochet, double crochet etc… for as many rows you need to fit comfortably on your head.

Step 17

As you continue to add rows as shown in the image. You hat will continue to increase in size. Keep going until you have reached the desired length you want for your head.

If you are working on the hat for a child, continue using the same methods for the desired length you want for the child's head.

Tip: I usually stop when the hat has reached a little bit underneath my earlobe, so I can add a crochet band of 3 or 4 rows. (Optional)

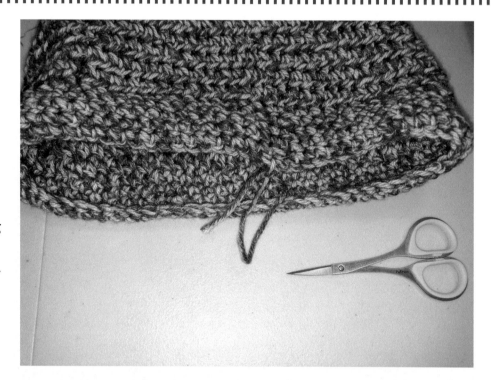

Step 18

If you look closely at this image, I have mad 4 rows of single crochet for the band of the hat.

When you finish adding all your rows, including your single crochet rows. Pull the yarn through the loop to lock.

Threading the Needle.

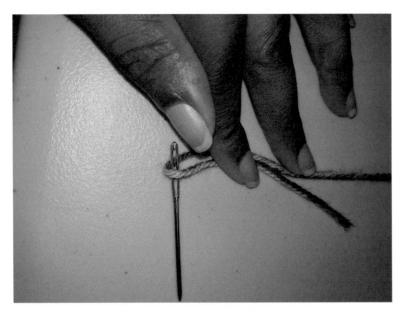

To thread your needle fold the tail end of your yarn over the eye of the needle as shown.

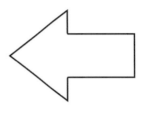

Pinch the yarn with your index finger and thumb as shown in the image.

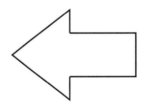

Push the yarn through
the eye of the needle and
slide the needle down till
it's snug on your yarn.

Just as shown here in the image.

Weaving in Ends

Weaving in the ends of the yarn is just as simple and easy as threading your needle.

Simply take the threaded portion of your yarn, and weave the tail end
through your completed work. Just as shown in the images below.

When you have completed weaving in the tail end of your yarn.

Tie off and cut off the excess yarn.

Follow this step for either size of the hat you are making.

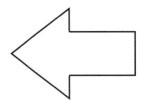

Weave yarn through the stitches of your project for a more secure closure, and tie off.

Just as shown in the images below.

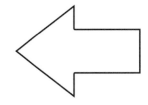

Continue to pull yarn
through stitches.

As shown in the image.

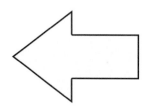

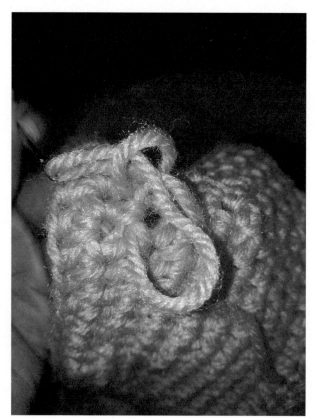

Make a knot and tie off just as
shown in the image.

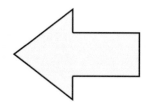

Tie off the end of your
tail, for a completed hat.

Completed Hat for An Adults Head

Adult and Child's Hat

I really hope you enjoyed
following along with making a
hat with me. I hope you enjoy
wearing it much, much more!

Printed in the United States
by Baker & Taylor Publisher Services